GRIEVE UPWARDS

One Man's Journey Through the Valley

by

David Schaeffer

CHI–Books
PO Box 6462
Upper Mt Gravatt Brisbane
QLD 4122
Australia

www.chibooks.org
publisher@chibooks.org

Grieve Upwards
One Man's Journey Through the Valley

Copyright © 2014 by David Schaeffer

Print ISBN: 978-0-9875608-7-2
eBook ISBN: 978-0-9875608-8-9

Under International Copyright Law, all rights reserved. No part of this Book may be reproduced, stored in a retrieval system, or transmitted in any form, including by any means electronic, mechanical, photocopying or otherwise in whole or in part without permission in writing from the publisher, except in the case of sermon preparation, reviews or articles and brief quotations embodied in critical articles. The use of occasional page copying for personal or group study is permitted and encouraged. Permission will be granted upon request.

Unless otherwise indicated, scripture is taken from the HOLY BIBLE, New American Standard – NASB Bible Copyright (c) 1960, 1962, 1963, 1968, 1971, 1972, 1973, 1975, 1977, 1995 by The Lockman Foundation, La Habra, Calif. All rights reserved.

Scripture quotations marked NLT are taken from the Holy Bible, New Living Translation, copyright (c) 1996, 2004. Used by permission of Tyndale House Publishers, Inc., Wheaton, Illinois 60189. All rights reserved.

Printed in Australia, United Kingdom and the United States of America.

Distributed globally via a range of outlets like: Ingram Book Group, Amazon USA, UK and Canada, BookDepository.com (UK) and others. Also in the USA via Spring Arbor – Christian Alliance nationwide and Barnes & Nobel. Also in the UK and Europe through Wesley Owen / Koorong UK. Available in Canada through outlets like Chapters, and also in Australia via Koorong.com.

Global eBook distribution through: Amazon Kindle, Apple iBookstore, Koorong.com, Wesley Owen (UK), Barnes & Nobel NOOK, Sony eReader, KOBO and others.

Editorial assistance: Anne Hamilton
Cover design: Dave Stone
Layout: Jonathan Gould

WHAT OTHERS ARE SAYING ABOUT THIS BOOK ...

Disappointment, loss and pain unfortunately are an inevitable part of life's journey. How we respond to these times can be crucial to our next season. David's journey through this book will prepare you to deal with these situations, or, if you are in the middle of tragedy and loss, this is your pathway through. The best book I have ever read about dealing with grief.

Mark Ramsey
Senior Pastor, Citipointe Church, Brisbane, QLD, Australia

What a beautiful and inspiring book! I already knew David and Tuula Schaeffer's story – at least in part – but in this book David takes us behind the public face of grief and loss.

Thank you, David for being so transparent! Your openness will help many people journey out of loss as they learn to "grieve upwards". I would recommend this book to anyone who has suffered loss, is trying to support someone else in loss – well, actually, everyone should read it!

Geoff Woodward
Senior Pastor, Metrochurch, Perth, WA, Australia

Life is lived forward and understood backwards. This book by David Schaeffer specifically deals with significant seasons of grief over many years. It arms the reader with timeless principles and understanding for life's journey. Everyone has a variety of grief experiences throughout life and the chapter on the flooding Clarence River is worth the read on its own. Take your time and absorb rather than race through. Highlight the passages that stand out to you and review them often. This book is a gem. Enjoy.

Chris Freeman
Founder, Balanced Wealth Creation, Newcastle, NSW, Australia

It was the somewhat counter-intuitive title *Grieve Upwards* that first caught my attention and having reached the third chapter, I could not put the book down until I had completely read it. Even then I found myself going back to reflect on David Schaeffer's phrase in Chapter 9, "God is far more concerned with our destiny, than He is with our happiness."

In my forty-five years of ordained life I have experienced countless occasions of being engaged with pastoring people in palliative care; conducting a multitude of funerals, and counselling and supporting the bereaved. Having read many books and documents on the subject of grief, I can wholeheartedly commend *Grieve Upwards* to any person experiencing bereavement and indeed, to those who walk with them in family life and in friendship. *Grieve Upwards* lives into the words of Scripture in the 1 Peter 1: verses 3 to 9. It is one of the most authentic, lucid, relevant and passionate books on responding to death and grief I have ever read.

The Right Reverend Richard Hurford
OAM, Retired Anglican Bishop, State Chaplain St John Ambulance, NSW, Australia

Since the days when David Schaeffer opened his heart to Christ at a Billy Graham crusade in 1968, his life has been the means of pointing other lives on the path to hope and freedom found in Jesus Christ. In his book *Grieve Upwards,* David allows us into the depths of the pain of his grieving the loss of his precious wife Marilyn, and beautiful daughter Belinda. Despite the despair and the utter darkness of those days, David's honesty and transparency is apparent as he guides us through the dark shadows of his own painful experience, to help us see that while grief is inevitable, it is possible to grieve with hope, to know that the dark valley of despair is not a dead–end, but is indeed a path to a renewed life. To read this book is an enriching experience; it is filled with a wisdom that is the product of bitter experience; and just like David's life, it points those whose lives have been weighed down by the overwhelming loss of a loved one, to a new dawn of a brighter and more meaningful future.

Major (Dr) Kelvin Alley
National Secretary, The Salvation Army National Secretariat, Australia

Grieve Upwards is a real man's journey through real pain. I am privileged to know David and to have known Marilyn and to see how as a husband and as a family they navigated through this extremely painful season. It was truly inspiring. God never promised that he would save us from suffering but that He would save us through it, and this book is all about the through.

Ross Abraham
Lead Pastor, Elevation Church, INC Chairman, Oceania

I walked with David in the weeks and months after the death of firstly, his wife and then ten years later his daughter. I observed first hand how he walked with joy and victory through those days. This is a man who has allowed his heart to be healed and who now has a testimony of light and life.

David's story gives amazing insights into the journey of grief, applicable to relational loss, personal loss, or any other kind of loss. His personal testimony will inspire you. Take the principles in this book and put them to work in your own circumstances. Thank you David. I congratulate you for the journey you have walked, and for wanting others to experience this measure of victory

David McDonald
Senior Minister, Empower Church Sydney, Past National Chairman, Christian Outreach Centre, Australia

What are the chances of my and David and Marilyn Schaeffer's paths crossing at the exact moment they needed to know they were in the palm of God's hand when they felt they were in the grip of uncertainty? I had no idea the message I brought to them that night could help them so much through the following three years. Whilst some may dwell on what they have lost when they pass through a season of grief, David paradoxically describes in his book *Grieve Upwards* how he gained. This book is both hopeful and helpful. I know you'll be blessed as you read it.

Phil Pringle
Founder and President, C3i Global

When I met David, he had already suffered extensive grief and then was thrust right back into it again but, despite this, I found him to be one of the most positive, forward-thinking and inspirational men I have ever met. For me, he offers great companionship and has an enthusiastic view of the future that is full of hope and excitement.

Grieve Upwards is an inspiration that details his journey from the depths of darkness and despair to seeing the light at the end of the tunnel and then out the other side. David offers helpful practical guidance and words of advice that are frank at times, yet gentle and persuasive.

Grieve Upwards will help you understand the feelings and emotions that you are going through and encourages you to take the time you need to grieve and share, and to continue to live life to the fullest. Any man, particularly those who think that they can grieve alone, should read this book.

Mark Kliner
Chief Executive Officer, Keller Australia Group of Companies

An amazingly brave and transparent look into one of the toughest journeys in someone's life in the loss of loved ones. Thank God for men like Dave who open up and talk about issues that most people (especially males) are too afraid to approach or even know how to deal with. Dave has been one of my heros over the years and this book has just elevated him to another level in my eyes. Thanks mate for sharing your story and journey with so many. You are a champion.

Andy Gourley
CEO and Founder, Red Frogs Australia

CONTENTS

	Acknowledgements	9
	Foreword	11
	Introduction	13
Chapter 1	Shocked	15
Chapter 2	Burn or Bury?	25
Chapter 3	God, You're a Wife Killer!	33
Chapter 4	How Males and Females Grieve Differently	39
Chapter 5	Questions and More Questions	45
Chapter 6	Unknowingly Prepared	57
Chapter 7	Avoiding Temptation While Grieving	65
Chapter 8	Choosing a Mate Second Time Around	71
Chapter 9	Trusting God Again	79
Chapter 10	Grieve Upwards	83
	Epilogue	91
	Endnotes	92

"I walked a mile with Pleasure;

She chatted all the way;

But left me none the wiser

For all she had to say.

I walked a mile with Sorrow;

And ne'er a word said she;

But, oh! The things I learned from her,

When Sorrow walked with me."

Robert Browning Hamilton

ACKNOWLEDGEMENTS

I had no idea when I began asking others to read and comment on the original manuscript how much valuable help I would receive. Some of those who have read these pages have been grammatical geniuses while others have provided insights far beyond my own personal capacity. Others asked questions and provided professional advice beyond my qualifications.

Your wisdom, encouragement, comments, suggestions and practical advice were all taken seriously and the book is better by far for your input.

A special thank you to all the members of my intimate and extended family. The stories are real, transparent and occasionally "raw". Your permission to share our journey with a wider audience, with people we will never meet and help along life's journey, is deeply appreciated. Matt, Sarah, Rach, Nate and Ro, you will always be dearer to me than breath itself.

My greatest encourager in life is my wife Tuula. It could have been difficult for her to read stories concerning Marilyn but, plainly put, she is bigger than that. We are both incredibly grateful for a second chance at love. We can make no comparison between our first and second marriages, simply because none is possible. Thank you, sweetheart.

David Schaeffer
www.davidschaeffer.com.au

FOREWORD

Growing up, it never occurred to me I would experience the loss of loved ones in my first 36 years to the extent I did. Then again, I suppose none of us do.

Grieving is one of the toughest experiences we encounter in life and it's not a matter where we get a choice. Rather, it is thrust upon us and our only option is to go through it. We can become stronger for it, however, if we're willing to get the right people around us, receive wise counsel and act upon it.

In dealing with my losses over the years, I count myself extremely blessed to have had Dad there to guide me through. When Mum passed away in 2003, he decided we, as a family, were not about to let this heart–wrenching loss hamstring our lives. Rather, we were going to embrace the journey we found ourselves on, and come out the other side stronger and healthier.

When my sister passed away in 2012, he gathered up the family once again and led us through our initial grief with a wisdom and grace that exceeded our expectations. All the more remarkable when you consider he had just lost his daughter.

His strength, steadfastness, faithfulness and resolve to remain the victor rather than the victim, no matter what happens in life, has been a great inspiration to me and many others. Because of his leadership, learning the lessons of grief has been a much easier process than it otherwise would have been. I can say that my faith and trust in God is stronger for it.

While the following pages represent one man's journey—and every journey is unique—I encourage you to take on board the wisdom presented here and experience first–hand just how valuable it is.

Matthew Schaeffer
Project Manager ARV

INTRODUCTION

"One day we will understand why this is the best thing that could have happened to us."

Those were the first words that came from my mouth. Where did they come from?

> Unscripted.
>
> Unexpected.
>
> Unrehearsed.

I looked into the eyes of my two daughters who, with me, had just helplessly watched on as their mother and my wife, ceased breathing with one laboured, exhaling sigh.

In that moment, Marilyn's body had surrendered to death, and her spirit surrendered to life.... into the safe arms of Jesus, and away from ours.

Fast–forward approximately ten years.

Belinda, one of the two daughters who, a decade previously, had stood at her mother's bedside, now lay in the intensive care section in

Sydney's Royal Prince Alfred hospital. Four years earlier, this had been the very place where she had received the gift of a liver transplant.

A grieving family somewhere in Australia had given permission for that organ to be taken from the dying body of their loved one and placed into Belinda's dying body to give it life.

Now a rare and aggressive cancer was sweeping through her body like a firestorm. Its rapid advance had been made possible by an immune system, purposefully lowered to prevent her body from rejecting the new liver.

Rohan had been my son–in–law for an agonisingly brief fifteen months. Together, we watched numbly as the life support machines were turned off one by one. At 32 years of age, Belinda took the same safe passage into eternity her mother had taken ten years earlier.

How does one go through experiences like this and rise again to a new normal, richer and stronger for the experience?

Read on...

CHAPTER ONE
SHOCKED

"A downer on the way up always trumps an upper on the way down."

The reality I had refused to accept was upon me. Right up until the last day, I had resisted reconciling myself to the thought Marilyn would die. Four or five days before, the doctor came to our home and, after examining her, drew me aside. He warned me she would deteriorate very quickly.

It is very easy to brush aside advice you don't want to receive, especially when you have been resisting it for three years. Even when Marilyn had agreed to be included in a cancer research trial, we quite quickly weeded out who we would and wouldn't listen to.

There was one professor at Newcastle's Mater hospital who had the sensitivity of a surgeon with a chainsaw. After just one visit with him, we went straight to our GP and suggested the guy had missed his calling and that he should have been an undertaker. What a meatloaf, albeit an educated one.

There was another doctor we decided not to put on our Christmas card list either. In asking us whether we would choose whole brain radiotherapy, he adding that, even though my beautiful wife was going to die, this treatment would enable her to live longer—as a vegetable. Realising the treatment he suggested was like shoving your head in an oven and cooking it for 40 minutes every day for six weeks, we chose to place our future into the hands of Almighty God.

We decided, that whether God's plans for us were miraculous intervention or resurrection, either way we'd do our best to stare down our Goliath.

I didn't know it then and, despite our best efforts to fight with the faith God gifted to us, I had begun pre-grieving.

This of course is what happens when people have a warning about imminent bereavement. Somewhere, deep down, without accepting my circumstances, I was committing myself to walking through this, even though the waters were deeper and blacker than I could survive on my own.

Our spirit knows what's up ahead long before our mind and soul catches on. It's not a premonition; it's a preparation so that our faith can rise to the impossible challenge.

Linn and Fabricant make this point: *"Often in our culture we are encouraged not to face grief but rather to deny our grief and 'be strong'."* [1]

Here's the thing; God, who knows the beginning from the end, who IS the beginning and the end, has gone before us and has prepared a way THROUGH these darkest of days. The faith He deposited in my heart was there for such a time as this.

Even through great releases of grief when I thought my sobs were turning me inside out, there was an underlying knowledge and hope that the journey was tilted upwards despite the emptiness and depression in my soul.

You may have had no chance to pre-grieve. You may have suddenly found yourself in a place where some fierce whirlwind has taken something of eternal and indescribable value from you. The same principle applies.

He knew!

As you trust yourself to Him, He will walk with you along a pathway that in no way took Him by surprise.

To further demonstrate this, let me tell you about the amazing events which occurred on the day Marilyn was diagnosed. She was told she had stage 4, amelanotic (colourless) melanoma on top of her head.

She had visited the cancer clinic the day before. I thought it was a regular check–up but, typically, she had procrastinated despite knowing of a rapid growth behind the hair line. She had also noticed some swelling of the glands in her neck.

I slept peacefully until morning, blissfully unaware Marilyn had stayed awake worrying and praying all night, waiting for me to stir. She made a cup of tea for us both, I suspect to help me fully awaken.

Without any explanation, she asked me to pray for her and seek God earnestly for a vision or prophecy, or any kind of word from Him. This had never happened before, and whilst I sensed her uneasiness, I let it ride and did my best. What did I see? A really bright future for her. I had no sense of the crisis threatening us. In the words of the prophet Elisha: *"Let her alone, for her soul is troubled within her; and the Lord has hidden it from me and has not told me."* (2 Kings 4:27)

That day became an intense and emotionally draining experience. The biopsy from the day before produced the worst possible result. Then the fine needle biopsy later that afternoon into the lymph glands of her neck indicated the cancer was on the move. Not knowing what to do and wondering how to tell our three children, we decided to attend a Church meeting that night where Phil Pringle, the founder of the great C3 Movement of Churches, was ministering.

Only Marilyn and I—not another soul—knew our situation when he called us out to pray for us. I still carry this prophecy around with me and declare it for encouragement and strength every now and then.

Here is an excerpt. *"You are going to bite into something new. You will bite that thing so hard, and you wont let it go. The devil is going to try and wrestle it off you and he will try to attack you from two angles. Physically and another angle. And the power of God is on you to grow through that trial."*

No one wakes up one morning anticipating that by the end of the day they will be in a life–and–death struggle, being stretched WAY beyond their elastic limit. That's the situation we found ourselves in, but we were able to end the day with not only this gargantuan challenge, but with an assurance that it was all in the master plan for our lives.

I could *never* have predicted a trial of that magnitude where the stakes would be so high. In the end, Marilyn was lifted into the waiting arms of God after fighting bravely for three years. I experienced a slow six–year resurrection, following an experience I can only describe as a living death.

But God knew everything BEFOREHAND. That knowledge came back time and again to reassure us that we could trust Him no matter what.

If you haven't yet entered into a personal relationship with Jesus Christ, the facts are still the same. He knew everything in advance for you too. And, even in the midst of your pain, if you invite Him in, He will come in and immediately commence strengthening you and leading you towards your new, healthy "normal".

Where was God when *you* needed Him? Patiently waiting in the shadows for you to turn and invite Him in. He has been one hundred percent available the whole time. Turn to Him, acknowledge you are a sinner unworthy of His forgiveness and invite Him in. Do it, it's urgent and He's ready.

I learned a really valuable lesson towards the end of our three-year trial. Marilyn was diagnosed on 28 September 2000 and went home on 3 June 2003. It wore me down, fighting in every way I could and not seeing any improvement for my efforts.

We had reached the stage where she was more-or-less a body covered with skin, unable to walk. So I carried her around the house when I couldn't push her in our five wheeler office chair. (Who WAS the genius that decided to build a split-level home?)

I knew many of the faith principles...you know... "I'm not moved by what I see, but what I believe."

However what I continually saw gave me a diminished ability to pray and seek God. These kinds of trial require huge doses of encouragement and replenishment. In the true spirit of Aussie mateship, David McDonald, then Australian Chairman for Christian Outreach Centre Churches, and his wife Tricia, would drop everything and drive from Sydney to Newcastle to support us.

The man is Caterpillar D9 bulldozer in prayer and, when he would begin to intercede and declare the victory Jesus won for us on the cross, I found I could find the face of God again.

This effect is like that which happens for birds flying in the 'V' wedge formation or with the *peloton* in the Tour de France. I discovered I could get in his slipstream.

Oh, the precious and altogether intimate moments I was able to spend with Him in the darkest of hours! I encourage many people engulfed in deep waters to slipstream behind another strong, Bible-confessing friend. Those times held me together and gave me supernatural strength for the darker days ahead. I remember people looking weirdly at me during the day of the funeral as if to say, "How can you be like this? You should be devastated."

Afterwards, I did a typically choleric thing and took a stab at how long it would take to get back on my feet. With no intelligent research or rational thinking, I gave myself two or three months to get better. In life, I had become quite proficient at diagnosing my own problems and prescribing foolproof remedies. Others might foolishly have needed to obtain long and hard–earned degrees before they could be trusted to help someone else in the same areas of need, but not me. I could fix myself. But...it didn't work.

I reasoned that, if I had a broken leg, I would go to the doctor. So, it stood to reason that, if I had a broken heart, I should see the appropriate doctor for that. Soon after bereavement, I took myself off to a recommended psychologist. After a variety of tests, he announced I was depressed. Convinced I was "normal", given my circumstances, I didn't return.

I'm sure now I could have really enriched my healing process if I had persisted a little longer. I am convinced the worst way to grieve is to retreat into the man cave and wait to feel better.

Not long into bereavement, I went to a leadership conference where the speaker made a comment that really put things in perspective. He said in effect: "Life is like this...four times out of five you will be carrying someone else on their stretcher. One time out of five, it will be your turn to be carried. When it IS your turn, make sure you're on it."

The lesson is that, while we may not need an army of supporters, we DO need a small number of committed people able to carry us through this season. What insanity causes us to think we can wade through this alone?

Don't be a mug, get on your stretcher and give yourself permission to grieve.

Of course, getting OFF the stretcher can be another experience entirely. When we are ON the stretcher—when we have given ourselves full permission to grieve—we typically engage with grief by rehearsing our experiences, and relating them to the present moment on life's journey.

I was doing this with a friend some five years after Marilyn's death, when he turned to me and said, "every time we speak, you rehearse Marilyn's death, and the effect grief has had on you. How long do you intend to keep this up?"

Well, anger was too small a word to describe how I felt. *How could he dishonour the memory of my wife like that?*

A sword through my heart would have been less painful. Troubled by my reaction, I resorted to taking it into my quiet place with God. It dawned on me in the stillness of those moments that it was time to get OFF the stretcher I had so willingly gotten ON five years earlier. It had grown comfortable up there. It was nice to have others carry you. It had become my 'life' for a season.

With unusual pain, I swung one leg and then the other over the edge and climbed down into a new life. From that moment I stopped rehearsing my painful experiences and began to embrace the future.

One symptom of grief I did NOT experience after Marilyn's death was denial.

I had had three years to process the growing reality that my wife was headed for distant shores. When it happened, I knew she was gone.

Was it a constant, mostly unspoken meditation for that whole three years? Of course it was.

However, near the end, while Marilyn was very ill but still coherent, she point–blank asked David McDonald: "Am I going to die?"

David was as encouraging as possible but, at that moment, we both knew we were going THROUGH this, not around it.

My wonderful son–in–law, Rohan, experienced intense denial after the death of his wife. He was married to Belinda for fifteen beautiful and tragically short months.

During the first eight months of bereavement he expected her to walk out of another room and convince him he was simply having a very bad dream. On one occasion, he couldn't find his mobile phone, so he rang the number using Belinda's phone. When he heard the ringtone and picked up his handset, he saw "Belinda" on his screen. His heart leapt, and in one wild moment he thought "I KNEW she was alive, I KNEW she was alive!"

Sleith sums it up like this: *"When we are overwhelmed emotionally by some event or loss, we protect ourselves psychologically by entering into a phase known as shock, numbness or denial."* [2]

These definitions of grief might help:

> \# Grief is the appropriate expression for loss
>
> \# Grief is the expression of loss for something or someone you can never replace
>
> \# Grief is the cost of loving someone
>
> \# Grief is like a huge carbuncle on your soul that seems to never empty no matter how often it is squeezed.

The definition that resonated clearly with me was: "Grief is the cost of loving someone."

Early into grief I was comparing notes with a young mum whose husband had tried to hang himself in the stairwell of their home. They got him down, but he was severely brain-damaged due to lack of oxygen. He lived on as a vegetable for the next year or so before dying.

"You had it easy," she exclaimed. And while it was true she had experienced unimaginable trauma, it was also true the love my wife and I shared had grown stronger and richer over thirty years, and then intensified beyond the Richter scale of human emotions during the final three.

Here's the truth. If we love someone deeply (as we should), there will be a great cost to it during grief, even if his or her death was a relatively peaceful experience.

When you finally decide that you would like to get better, make sure you have one or two experienced and understanding listeners who are genuinely committed to your recovery, no matter how long it takes.

You may not have reached that place yet, because the intense connection a person has to the one they lost has a great power of attachment. But one day, you look in heaven's direction and you give God permission to make you well again and establish a new normal. You cautiously open yourself to the future and its possibilities. That's a BIG moment!

Bowlby comments: *"The resolution of grief is not to sever bonds but to establish a changed bond with the dead person."* [3]

It is a defining moment when we withdraw permission to stay on the stretcher and give God permission to heal us...when we give ourselves permission to get better.... when we begin embracing the future again

Key thoughts

> \# The faith He deposited in your heart is there for such a time as this

> \# He knew in advance and as you trust yourself to Him, He will walk with you along a pathway that in no way took Him by surprise

> \# Where was God when you needed Him? Patiently waiting in the shadows

> \# When it's too hard to pray, get in someone else's slipstream

> \# The worst way to grieve is to retreat into your man cave and wait to feel better

> \# The more intense the connection a person has to the one they lost, the greater the power of attachment

\# While we don't need an army of supporters, we DO need a small number of committed people able to carry us at various times through this season

\# It is defining moment the day you withdraw permission to stay on the stretcher and grant permission to be made better

CHAPTER TWO
BURN OR BURY?

Between death and the funeral, everyone is faced with a choice that, when contemplated later, can have a jarring impact on the soul. Here in Australia we have only two choices regarding the body of the person we have held, loved, hugged, kissed, delighted in and admired. All through our married life, I thrilled to the touch of Marilyn's hand in mine. On some occasions I would phone her through the day simply to hear her voice.

But what are my choices now? To burn the body up or bury it down.

"How could I do that?" The questioned haunted me often. Both choices are rotten—one not better than the other.

How do we cope with this? As if we don't feel bad enough about ourselves and life already during this time.

This is how God helped me:

I was in a Sunday church meeting; the worship time was in full swing. I was in some agony at the thought I had cremated Marilyn's body. However, at the same time, I realised burying it seemed no better. In worship, I could "see" myself before His throne and became conscious of others near me. In my imagination, I saw myself with Abraham (died of old age), Paul (beheaded), Peter (crucified upside down), King David (old age) and Elisha (disease).

Somehow I knew Marilyn was amongst the crowd but seeing her would have distracted me from Jesus.

Marriage is an earthly, human experience, unnecessary in heaven. She had no further use of marriage...she was with her bridegroom and I was struggling without my bride. Seeing her in this vision would have been torturous, and Jesus spared me the pain.

I became content to let the reality of heaven and eternity wash over me and bring peace and freedom to my soul. It's the old saying about facts and truth. The fact is I cremated Marilyn. The truth is that she is alive and safely home. As I continued worshipping, I was reminded of a Bible passage I had grown to love over many years of reading:

> *"But you have come to Mount Zion and to the city of the living God, the heavenly Jerusalem, and to myriads of angels, to the general assembly and church of the firstborn who are enrolled in heaven, and to God, the Judge of all, and to the spirits of the righteous made perfect, and to Jesus, the mediator of a new covenant, and to the sprinkled blood, which speaks better than the blood of Abel."* (Hebrews 12:22–24)

Marilyn was amongst the "spirits of the righteousness made perfect" and I could see it clearly.

Afterwards, I wanted to encourage so many other grieving people, so I worded a Thank You card to say, "It meant so much to us that you would think of us and strengthen us in recent times. Marilyn is safe and well. Thank you for praying for us as we continue powerfully in our destiny."

Up to the time of the funeral, the support that grievers receive can be quite overwhelming. After the funeral, people disperse in planes, trains and cars. It can be a really unusual experience as we come to earth with a thud.

We can amaze ourselves with our ability to comfort others in the depth of our own grief. But soon enough, the anaesthetic of those early days... the numbness a soul experiences when it is bearing a pain it cannot tolerate... begins wearing off.

It is then that the true grieving experience cuts in.

There were some things I did really well when it came to those days. In hindsight, I believe we should happen to grief rather than grief happening to us.

What do I mean?

I mean, we don't have much strength during this season, but we can still make some quality choices and be in charge of the journey, rather than the journey being in charge of us.

Shortly after I decided I didn't need another visit to the psychologist, I also decided I needed something to continue helping myself, as well as the ones I loved most in the world: my kids Belinda and Rachel, and Matt and his wife Sarah.

Belinda was just completing university and Rachel was just completing high school. Matt was a qualified project manager. Is there any "good" age to lose your mum?

I phoned Hillsong Church in Sydney and asked for their counseling department. I reasoned that they were a big church and should therefore have many resources for people like me. I was referred to professional people who recommended a DVD series, *Griefshare*.

It is unwise for people recently bereaved to take the responsibility for helping others process their grief, and wisely, they almost refused to sell me the resource when they learned of my circumstances. After a serious discussion they relented and we exchanged money for a healing pathway. My kids initially got a real kick out of the old–fashioned clothing styles and haircuts. I didn't know about "frullets" until then. But soon enough, their wisdom, grace and gentleness of spirit washed over us all and we were on our way.

Sometimes it takes months, even years before a person is ready to begin processing their grief in this way.

Problem one: I was a grieving choleric. Now a choleric (do it now!) when devoid of wisdom, would rather make a bad decision quickly than a good decision slowly.

Well, grief had accounted for the small amount of wisdom I possessed. So I set up "family night" every Monday night.

Just as an aside, it is extremely helpful to understand your behavioural style during a season of grief. I was ready to engage with a healing pathway, but my kids were at different places. I learned that everyone grieves differently and at his or her own pace. Unless you're doing things that bring harm, there is no right or wrong way. No prescription anyone has to follow. In fact, beware the person who hasn't experienced grief and thinks you should have "closure" by now. Also avoid the person who *has* experienced grief and wants to put their experience onto you.

Problem two: I had never learned to cook and family night involved a meal. I found a recipe book that had arrived with the oven about eight years earlier. I noticed that, if I learned to cook a roast, I would become accomplished at four meals—one for each type of meat. I also learned to cook apple crumble (no cheap rolled oats topping for me!) and nearly killed one of my good mates in the process. One of those family *Griefshare* nights, Tezza and Gaye came along also. Tezza was half way through his apple crumble when he yelled, "What's this!"

Reaching into his mouth he pulled out a large sliver of glass. It must have sheared off the inside of the ceramic dish when I knocked it in my hurry to get it in the oven.

On another occasion I gave myself the mother of all food poisoning experiences. At that time I learned that leftover baked vegetables don't stay fresh forever in the fridge. Surviving the experience and learning to cook was in some way therapeutic. A little step forwards, it felt good to be heading in the right direction.

The *Griefshare* DVDs came with a book to write in every day. It's a wonderful manual and it really scratched my itch. Some days I crawled out of bed at the crack of eleven a.m. Then sometimes for an hour, sometimes longer, I would engage with that day's page in the manual. The questions were so simple and the Bible passages so brief, it made it easy for me to pray and meditate. I felt like every morning this little book would gently take me by the hand and lead me to Jesus.

I'm not sure I would have had enough strength to do even that alone.

I made a note in my journal at that time: "It is very easy to starve yourself spiritually during grief just because of the shock and low motivation. It doesn't make sense to grieve AND starve at the same time, does it?"

My advice?

Find something or someone to gently lead you to Jesus at the start of every day. You will feel anchored again to the Rock that will not move.

One thing I felt keenly in the early alone days was the absence of someone with whom I could be totally transparent. I'm amazed many marriages don't cultivate this.

It's an enormous freedom to have someone listen to our innermost thoughts whether they make sense or not... whether they are reactions or responses... whether they are right or wrong or a mixture of both.

I only needed one good friend and, again, David McDonald was happy to see me any time. He listened mostly; I can't remember him giving much advice. The freedom to empty my thought tank and avoid bottling things up under intense pressure was essential. One authentic friend is worth fifty enthusiastic friends who unthinkingly declare: "Praying for you." You know they're not, but don't bother criticising them, they are simply not God's provision for you.

Grief has its lighter side. One thing many people don't know about grieving people is that they love to laugh. Some people eat lots more food than they should. I personally went on a shopping rampage. New things started to be carried in through the front door with such regularity Matt said to his sisters: "Someone take the cheque book off him!"

What was occurring? I was trying to have some sweet experiences in the midst of an otherwise bitter life.

On another occasion my beautiful second wife, Tuula, and I were conducting a *Griefshare* group on the Central Coast of NSW. Someone (guess who?) decided everyone should bring along a joke about death and grief. So there we were enjoying coffee and dessert, with jokes that were creating side–splitting belly laughs. Then we would watch the *Griefshare* DVD and tears of grief would roll down people's cheeks. They must have been totally exhausted by the end of the night, but they kept coming back for more.

Key Thoughts

> # It's the old saying about facts and truth. The fact is I cremated Marilyn. The truth is she is alive and safely home.
>
> # Be in charge of the journey, rather than the journey being in charge of you.
>
> # You can exchange money for a healing pathway.
>
> # It is extremely helpful to understand your behavioural style during a season of grief.
>
> # Unless you're doing things that bring harm, there is no right or wrong way to grieve.
>
> # Beware the person who hasn't experienced grief and thinks you should have "closure" by now.

\# Beware the person who has experienced grief and thinks you should follow their pattern.

\# Find something to gently lead you to Jesus at the start of every day. You will feel anchored again to the Rock that will not move.

\# One authentic friend is worth fifty enthusiastic unthinking friends. The freedom to empty your think–tank and avoid bottling things up under intense pressure is essential.

\# Grieving people love to laugh.

CHAPTER THREE
GOD, YOU'RE A WIFE KILLER!

Two or three months into bereavement, I was sitting downstairs in my Newcastle home, alone at the computer. Doing nothing but feeling immensely angry, alone, and sick and tired of feeling like there was no light at the end of the tunnel, I looked away to heaven and cried: "God, you're a wife–killer!"

No one could tell me how long this journey would take. Every other well–meaning person had his or her sickly platitudes. "Only the good die young." "She was too young to die." "God always picks the freshest flowers out of the garden." Give me a well–earned break!

Normally people love to talk about the ones they lost and still deeply love. A comment such as: "She was a wonderful person" or "She had a wicked sense of humour" can be all the invitation needed to bring comfort through refreshed memories.

"Tell me about …" can be another invitation the grieving person can accept or reject.

Following Marilyn's death, a colleague rang and began apologising for taking so long to contact me. "I didn't know what to say," he confessed.

My response was simple. "You make the call, I'll fill up the time." For me, I had an ocean of words waiting to carry the pain away.

Not every grieving person has the talking bug, however. Many times the mere presence of a friend is comfort enough. And if you talk about nothing long enough, you will usually end up talking about something. Solomon was onto this when he said:

> *"He who restrains his words has knowledge, and he who has a cool spirit is a man of understanding. Even a fool, when he keeps silent, is considered wise: when he closes his lips, he is considered prudent."* (Proverbs 17:27–28)

Do you know what I heard back from God after the outburst accusing Him of being a wife-killer?

Nothing. Absolutely nothing.

Do you think a cry of pain in one of His kids causes the Great Physician to recoil or draw near?

In those dark days, our souls are so wounded, most of us couldn't hear from God even if He shouted. We mostly need him to show up in another Christian, in human form. So, do you know what happened?

Within thirty minutes or so of pulling myself together, the phone rang. And who should be on the line but Major Kelvin Alley, a Salvation Army officer. He wasn't a Major then, but I loved and respected him like few others. We had grown close when we were both pastoring local churches in Port Macquarie on the mid-north coast of NSW. I regarded him as the humblest and most loving man I have ever known. To have Kelvin ring right at that moment felt like God himself was reaching out for me with his soft loving arms. I can remember being unable to speak much but, as I listened to his voice, my heart once again melted in gratitude and love for God.

One of the wonderful things asked in the *Griefshare* manual is: "What or who is at the centre of your universe?"

It points out that if anyone or anything besides Jesus is there, they will all die. People die. Pets die. Cars depreciate. Houses deteriorate. Possessions are superseded. The quickest way to lose our mental and emotional equilibrium in a time of grief is to lose the centre of our world. You can see what I'm getting at. With Jesus at the centre, we will never feel un–centred, even at the darkest moments of our lives.

Please let me challenge you: work out what is temporary and what is permanent and arrange your life around those truths.

Long before Marilyn died, we visited our solicitor to arrange our will. It was just a normal, responsible thing to do.

When it was our turn to go in to his office, Michael appeared shaken. "I've just had a terrible experience. The lady who just in before you told me she only had three months to live."

"Michael," I asked, "how many people are in this room?"

"Three," he replied.

"And how many are dying?" I asked.

Without answering, he took in the question and, after a period of quietness, said: "Thank you. You must help a lot of people."

Being properly centred.... Christ–centred...goes a long way to helping us think correctly at times when life is turned on its ear. Michael had been given perspective and it comforted him.

Perspective in life is a great asset. According to what we are exposed to in life, we develop a philosophy of life, a big–picture idea of how it all fits together.

One essential perspective is that we live our lives against the backdrop of eternity. It's too late to argue the point on this one. There IS an eternity to live beyond mortality. Christianity is just a bunch of unanswered questions and unproven statements unless Jesus rose from the dead, proving eternal existence.

There is a vast amount of historical evidence that points to Jesus rising from the dead. However the most conclusive evidence is uncovered when ordinary people like us open our hearts, seek His forgiveness, invite Him in and discover, years later, our lives have been altered permanently for the better.

How could a dead God achieve that? What was once a dead religion is now the most intimate and honest of relationships.

Why is grieving such a painful experience?

I learned one answer to this lesson years before Marilyn died. Matt, as a teenager, had had his heart broken by a girl for first time. "Why does it hurt so much?" he asked through tears.

It was one of those times when truth came out of my mouth before I had planned the answer. "Because the pictures in your inner world are different to the pictures in your outer world."

Matt's imagination was full of pictures of an attractive girl. But in reality she had walked out of his life. His physical eyes couldn't see what the eyes of his imagination were still seeing clearly.

Now, multiply that by a gazillion and that's the multiplied pain of the emotional conflict—or some may prefer to call it *torment*—when a soul mate dies. Kubler–Ross and Kessler make this poignant comment:

> "A new relationship begins. We learn to live with the loved one we lost... trying to put back the pieces that have been ripped away." [4]

For me, a page in the book of life had been ruthlessly turned to a new chapter. Everything had been thrown up in the air and questions that had been answered long ago (such as "Who would I marry?") rushed back to confront me. If I was ever to re–marry, I certainly didn't need a new wife in the bed and two wives in my head!

I detected an ominous, lengthy journey ahead during which these things would be resolved.

It is the age–old conundrum. We are all born, we all die and we all live forever.

Christians are caught between living for a God who promises miracles and healing, and guarantees death.

When we reconcile these two things, we finally realise that one day, we will *not* be healed. Disease, for instance, took the life of the prophet with a double portion of Elijah's anointing. Go figure!

Remember, marriage is much more than a "relationship." It is a COVENANT, where a male and a female consummate their marriage by enjoying sexual intercourse. That's where God makes two people into one and, if you invite Him, becomes the third person in your marriage. No wonder there is pain at death! Your covenant bond is ripped away, leaving a bruised and bleeding soul.

Key Thoughts

Do you think a cry of pain in one of His kids causes the Great Physician to recoil or draw near?

Christians are caught between living for a God who promises miracles and healing, and guarantees death

Marriage is far more than a relationship, it is a covenant. The essential nature of covenant is not a temporary contract but a permanent oneness.

CHAPTER FOUR
HOW DO MALES AND FEMALES GRIEVE DIFFERENTLY?

Let me state categorically no two people are the same. Any attempt to stereotype the way males and females grieve will be met by someone whose experience defies any scientific or non–scientific assessment of the grieving journey. Some females will read the description for males and feel more aligned with that than the one for females... and vice versa. Furthermore, there are some days when we may fit the so–called "male" way, and other days when we may fit the "female" way.

The grieving experience can be compared to Melbourne's weather. "Is it beach weather today?" one Melbournian will ask another.

"Wait a minute," answers the other.

When grief surfaces like a whale coming up for air, some trigger has caused it to rise. A thought, a picture, a phone call, an object, a comment... a whole host of little things can press the grieving button.

Rather than progress through the emotional symptoms of grief in orderly stages, we may experience them in a chaotic and unpredictable format. Anger, tears, doubt, laughter, relief, faith, confusion, cynicism, hope, confidence—the powerful surge of emotions circulating our souls can make for an exhausting day.

Dunn and Leonard describe this perfectly. *"The unpredictable timing and odd combinations of emotions that hit you during grief can leave you confused and despairing."*[5]

Here are some differences between males and females that *could* cause them to grieve differently.

Males are largely ego–driven. Generally, their greatest emotional need is acceptance and respect. So when a male hears something that endorses his worth and value, it is a boost to his self–esteem and morale.

At some stage in early grief, I was sitting with the friend I had made myself accountable to, musing out loud what would become of me now. His answer was a throwaway line for him, but it was something that charged my batteries. I experienced a lift in my hope levels as if I had just downed a shot of barley green.

"David, we believe in you." That was all he said.

He affirmed my value. It sounded like I wasn't going to be detoured into pit lane for an extended overhaul. For me, it was a moment of unexpected hope. No wonder the Bible says the power of life and death is in the tongue.

Females, on the other hand are largely emotion–driven. Generally their greatest emotional need is security. They love feeling safe. Females feel safe when they are financially secure, when they know their children are safe, when they feel safe spiritually, when they have friends who will patiently listen.

How many words does a woman have in her every day? Multiply that by umpteen, and that's the new number in a season of grief. Trusted friends of the same sex are vital for a woman.

It would be unwise for a male to become a grieving woman's listener. Verbal intercourse is possibly the most powerful form of foreplay for many women. It is far more powerful than sexual intercourse and one thing can easily lead to another. Grief presents its own range of vulnerabilities. Apart from this, the sheer volume of her words could overwhelm him. These are generalities, but they carry some important principles.

One strong variation of these principles can occur when grief follows a highly traumatic incident. Then emotional and verbal shutdown can be easily experienced.

In this instance, there can be little difference between a male and female's response. I have endeavored to help people make progress following a suicide, only to discover they have extreme difficulty processing it internally or verbally. Pain deeper than deep can cause our engines to seize.

Males are generally ready to 'move on' more quickly than females. This can be for a number of reasons—quite apart from simply being hardwired as a male. His sex drive can be amplified at this time rather than minimised. Usually, the most powerful way a male receives acceptance is through making love with his wife. She lovingly gives what he considers to be one of the most precious things he can receive from her. It is as if she is saying to him: "You are so valuable to me… you are worth so much to me, I want to give my whole self to you without holding anything back."

That may not be what SHE is thinking, but the message HE receives is unmistakable!

Females can play the *but–what–if* game much longer than males. Men can consider the same questions, but are quicker to resolve them with *but–it–didn't–and–it–can't* and move on.

Let me repeat: no two males grieve the same way, and no two females. Further to that, our logic can be all over the place as we try to fathom the unfathomable. Male or female, our confidantes need to be non–

judgmental, understanding that our ability to reason things through correctly will improve over time.

Let me illustrate. During one *Griefshare* small group session, one participant—a new widow having a really rough patch—sprayed everyone in the room with, "I'm SO over this! God doesn't care! I don't think He even exists!"

Before any of our budding theologians could give her the benefit of their wisdom, I stated: "Well it's official, there is no God."

It validated the griever's right to be on her own journey and grieve in her own way. The pain was speaking, not the griever. She didn't believe what she said any more than the imprisoned John the Baptist believed himself when he momentarily doubted Jesus' identity:

> "Now when John, while imprisoned, heard of the works of Christ, he sent word by his disciples and said to Him, 'Are You the Expected One, or shall we look for someone else?'"
> (Matthew 11:2–3)

In that moment during the small group meeting, we created a safe environment for someone to take another step along the path. After about thirty minutes she had regained her equilibrium.

My personal experience was that I needed only one or two confidantes. My inner thoughts were not available for publication in those early days when I was trying bravely to walk forwards through the wet mud of grief. Many females happily express their inner emotions to many more listeners.

One reason for this is the cultural weakness in the Aussie male where he tends to isolate, rather than share his journey with trusted companions. I had a river of words in me, but rather than speak these out, I journalled them and poured out my thoughts privately.

A really helpful thing to assist us in accepting ourselves as we grieve is to understand our behavioral style—or our personality type.

Cholerics like to be in control and love to get things done. No wonder grief is so tough for them! How far out of control of life can you be during the initial stages of bereavement? I confess to being one of these and, as stated previously, I initially gave myself two or three months to get through the grief process. This personality type is never better illustrated than by my unreasoned and unreasonable prediction. Needless to say, when this time had elapsed, I still felt like road kill.

Sanguines love acceptance and approval and are highly vulnerable to rejection. Our soul easily mistakes grief for rejection, so the spiral into grief is very easy for these personality types. Remember, we accept what we understand and reject what we don't. Why add self-rejection to grief for no sensible reason when a little understanding about ourselves could relieve a lot of emotional pressure? It can even cause us to laugh at ourselves occasionally!

Phlegmatics are loyal for life and hate feeling unsafe. What a double whammy grief is for a phlegmatic! Is *this* the reward for a lifetime of loyalty? Grief for them is the ultimate wound for the soul. Recovery can be slow without the benefit of understanding themselves.

Melancholics are creative types who rely on devising a "secure" plan before going to work. They resist change (especially sudden change) with the enthusiasm of a child on their first day at school. These wonderful people are really knocked for six if bereavement is unexpected. Alternatively, if death was a lengthy process, they have plenty of time to self-depress (or adjust if they understand themselves).

No matter what we learn, our grief experience will still be totally unique. I have discovered you cannot "batch process" people through grief. A good grief coach should understand this and provide the necessary help.

Key Thoughts

Any attempt to stereotype the way males and females grieve will ultimately fall short.

\# We often experience the symptoms of grief in a chaotic and unpredictable format.

\# Generally, a male's greatest emotional need is acceptance and respect.

\# Generally a female's greatest emotional need is security.

\# Verbal intercourse is far more powerful than sexual intercourse.

\# When grief is the result of high-level trauma, emotional and verbal shutdown can be easily experienced.

\# We should be non–judgmental listeners for a grieving person, because often it is the pain doing the talking.

\# Understanding your personality type can help you avoid self–rejection during grief.

CHAPTER FIVE
QUESTIONS AND MORE QUESTIONS

As time passes, many questions, some valid and some unanswerable, cross your mind. Questions like:

 # Could I have done more to prevent what happened?

The answer for this in hindsight is often 'yes', but we don't have the benefit of hindsight at the time. There's no crystal ball where we can see the future. We become as smart as Einstein with hindsight! It is an especially bad question to entertain because it has a great capacity to bring guilt—a horrible commodity that doesn't need to be added to the depression we are already experiencing.

My advice? Knock it on the head.

How?

This is what I do. Sometimes in the mail, we receive forms to fill out that look like they require a degree in rocket science to understand. Knowing they won't go away by ignoring them, I find someone with more wisdom and patience to attend to them. That's exactly what I did with the "too hard to answer" questions during grief. A beautiful piece of advice found in 1 Peter 5:7 encourages us to cast all our cares onto the Person who is caring for us.

Go ahead.

We are His personal project during grief, and His care is large enough to cater for all our unanswerables. He has a good filing system and our questions won't be lost.

How do I cope with unfulfilled sexual desires?

When a man's mate dies, it can be an abrupt transition from a regular sex life to zero. For others, it becomes impossible to continue a sexual relationship at some point because of his mate's deteriorating health. In any case, the question is there. Think of it this way...

Our bodies are electricity companies, food processing plants, movie theatres, plus a host of other things. They are also chemical factories.

When we first become sexually active, chemicals begin flowing around our bodies that demand sexual satisfaction two or three times a week. This varies from person to person, of course. However every male I have discussed this with admits to a strong dose of sexual frustration if these chemicals are denied their natural expression.

So before we think of this question morally, think of it chemically. What can we do to cope with sexual frustration after bereavement?

>Grin and bear it...tough it out.

>Have an affair.

>Engage the services of a prostitute.

>Turn to internet relationships.

I don't recommend ANY of these things. However, don't be surprised at some people's choices when depression, low wisdom and high frustration combine to provide their own brand of desperation. All of these choices have potentially nasty and painful consequences.

If a man has had a rich and satisfying sexual relationship, one payoff for him was comfort. A male's greatest emotional need is acceptance, and one of the most powerful sources of acceptance is when his wife accepts him into her body.

The result? The man feels greatly accepted... and comforted.

In the midst of grief, men NEED comfort, so the question becomes how to get it. Is masturbation an option?

Instead of providing an answer, I have to leave you with a question. No one answer can satisfy every person, because there is a moral consideration to this as well as a chemical one. Here is the question...

What does the Bible say?

Now don't switch off if you're not a Bible reader. There are plenty of people who are, and who are willing to help.

Thomas Campbell once wisely said: "We speak where the Bible speaks, and are silent where the Bible is silent." So what does it or does it NOT say?

Many people have a personal value system that gives rise to very powerful opinions. I have heard very powerful opinions about this question, many from people who have never journeyed through this, and have never had to wrestle with sexual frustration following bereavement. However, if we search, the answers are there in the Bible in the same way they are there for every other aspect of life.

We don't have to search alone. Find a grief–coach or consult specialists and counsellors in this field to help formulate decisions that rest easy in the soul; decisions that provide no condemnation to the heart.

> # Should I sell the house?
> # When should I start dating again?
> # When should I clean out the wardrobe?

These three questions are somehow linked in my mind, especially if you have children— whether they are living with you or not. "Never make a big decision when you are under pressure." I don't know who said it first, but I wish I could remember it more often.

Sell the house?

We may be tempted to make a new start ASAP but, if you've had a happy home, think of it like this. You've just lost the most valuable thing in the world. Do you seriously want to add to that loss by deleting the environment that holds so many precious memories for you?

That choice can give you a double whammy. Are you sure you need that?

And more importantly, do your kids need that? Are they ready to wave that part of their life goodbye too?

My advice? Ask them. Ask the kids. They will help you find wisdom.

Dating?

Some men are just the marrying kind. In fact, the Bible goes so far as to say that celibacy is a gift. It certainly doesn't reside at my address. Some never re–marry. Some put it off for some time. But don't think you are somehow dishonoring your deceased mate if these desires surface in the ensuing months (this can be quite a large contrast with widows).

Please, please, please, don't handle this on your own. You MUST have a confidante who can wisely caution and modify your thinking.

When, and if, you get interested in someone, be transparent with someone wiser and detached from your emotions.

Again the best barometer for your thinking can come from your kids. Are they ready to have another woman fill the vacancy yet? If they're NOT ready, how much family conflict are you creating? Remember, you have enough conflict already in your own soul without adding to it.

I remember casually connecting with a few girls on a social level. One of my daughters, Belinda, was never shy to tell me what she thought. "And the others feel this way too!" she would say to strengthen her case.

I knew better than to waken the sleeping tiger, so the cautions paid off. On Father's Day in 2004, thirteen months after Marilyn's death, my kids were visiting me on the Central Coast. After church, we went to an Italian restaurant for lunch. Once we had eaten, Matthew, the spokesman for the group, cleared his throat in preparation for an important announcement. "Dad, we've discussed it, and if you want to form a new relationship, you have our support."

Thank God I hadn't taken the matter into my own hands and forced my children into a relationship they would have violently, or worse passively, rejected. I had worked out I would only be ready for a new relationship when I had enough fuel in my tank to meet the other person's needs.

How many people jump quickly into a new relationship to fill the hole someone else left? Then they wonder where all the conflict comes from when the relationship is so lopsided. When we consider we are ready to meet someone else's physical, emotional and spiritual needs, it can be an indicator we have regained a measure of wholeness in ourselves.

Shortly after this, I received an email from Tuula. This was our first contact and began our journey to the altar in January 2006. In truth, despite giving me their blessing, the kids weren't ready even then, nor were Tuula's, but they bravely tried to adjust.

A last key thought on this one. In one sense, your kids may NEVER be ready for you to move into a new relationship.

So there is a time when you shouldn't for their sake and a time when you should. What do I mean? When enough water has flowed under the bridge, you may be faced with the responsibility of making sure they don't get stuck in grief.

Re–marrying tells everyone that, despite the pain of yesterday, you are moving forwards into your future. And the ultimate effect is that you inspire others to look and move in that direction too. Today, Tuula's and my kids celebrate those decisions despite the fact most of them initially recommended in no uncertain terms that we should wait for say... another year. We simply figured it was time for us AND them to get on with life.

When should I clean out her clothes from the wardrobe?

The first time I suggested this, my kids gave me a flat refusal. Don't be surprised if you're ready for this before them. So I left it, knowing that those clothes represented soooo much to us all, and stirred up very powerful memories. Some clothes were worn on special occasions; some were gifts, some fashions represented decades of associated memories. So I just closed that side of the wardrobe figuring it wasn't going to hurt anyone if they just sat there.

And in the fullness of time, they were ready. What a day! I discovered that, if you let this take its course, a day of sadness can become a day of celebration. My two girls, Bel and Rachel, saw an opportunity for dress–ups. Laughter, acting out how mum walked in this dress and shoes, shopping memories plus squeals of "I want to wear that one" filled the house. How my heart sang to see the kids celebrate their mum's life!

How do I know if I'm grieving properly?

The Bible clearly states we should grieve "with hope". Obviously then, there is a wrong way to do it. One of the reasons I enthusiastically engaged with *Griefshare* is because it had such wonderful Christians who had gone where I was going. They were willing to share truths that inspired hope for the future.

A favorite Bible verse for me in those days was Isaiah 42:3, *"...a bruised reed He will not break and a dimly burning wick He will not extinguish."*

Man, did that speak to me and provide hope! There are oodles of hope and buckets of comfort in the Bible. A friend of mine once said: "Open your bible, turn anywhere, it's all good!"

If you haven't been a Bible reader, what a perfect time to start. You have aches that only He can massage.

One of life's greatest keys is that we tend to accept what we do understand and reject what we don't understand. If we fail to understand the grieving process (which is a HEALING process) we could end up rejecting it because of the pain. And pain is the very thing God has provided for us to make us whole again.

One other wonderful key to help me grieve right was this. I developed and maintained one strong, consistent, simple confession I would say every day. You can work out your own, but mine was...

"Today, the Kingdom of God is experiencing a resounding victory, and the kingdom of darkness is experiencing a humbling defeat."

It became a constant in the midst of all my emotional fluctuations.

You can be honest in a way that helps overcome depression on a daily basis.

My encouragement? Try being honest about your future, rather than your present.

How long will the grieving process take?

When I grew up in Grafton on the far north coast of NSW, we lived on the banks of the mighty Clarence River. It is still called Big River Country. The Clarence has some of its headwaters right up in Queensland and, when rain falls in every catchment area, large floods can be experienced downstream in town.

When the Clarence was swollen, anything and everything would tear past our house in the murky and dangerous flood waters: cattle—living or dead and bloated—great clumps of hyacinth, trees, boats that had lost their mooring. You name it, it went past.

Before they built a levee bank around the town, we used to row dad to work along roads that cars had driven on just days before. For us kids, it was all excitement. Talk about cleaning out the river system!

Interestingly, a major grieving experience can unearth other previous grief experiences that have never been resolved. There can be a build-up of "stuff" in your own river.

As I was proceeding through *Griefshare*, one session showed a couple who had adopted a baby. They then discovered their new bub was HIV positive. The baby died and the adoptive mother experienced real anger towards the birth mother for allowing a little child to be born this way.

As this was playing out in front of me, I suddenly realised how angry I had been (and still was to a degree) towards the pastor of a very sick church where I had taken leadership after moving from my own beautiful church, my "baby", in Port Macquarie. Happily, the church in question was revived over time, and some of the most wonderful people in the world are still worshipping there.

The floodwaters of this grief over Marilyn's death were washing out the build-up of unresolved grief from previous years. I was able to give myself permission to grieve for the church and city I had committed myself to spirit, soul and body.

I remembered someone asking me after I preached once in the church I took over: "Why are you so angry?" At that moment, I knew.

When grieving, we can discover it's more about our lingering pain than about the one who died. Horrible wounds are left in the heart of the survivors.

And interestingly, it's the 'secondaries' that come to get you. The OBVIOUS loss is the person who died. There are many far less obvious losses that compound the experience. Like:

> Losing the expectation and ability to go on family holidays again.
>
> Grieving for your children who lost their mum.
>
> Losing the opportunity to work out another day of your destiny together.
>
> Losing the joy of visiting your in–laws for a peaceful break.

There can be lots to wash out of our river, so don't wonder that grieving can take a long time.

Should I bottle this up and be strong?

As I tried to answer this one, I had a look at how David (from the Bible) grieved when his best mate Jonathan was killed in battle. It helped when I saw that David took time out to bring his grief front and centre and powerfully engage with it.

We Aussies can easily follow the British culture and deny, avoid and keep a stiff upper lip. WRONG! David wept, fasted, mourned, openly demonstrated and spoke out his grief. Then he journalled his emotions and thoughts in a Bible passage commonly called *The Song of the Bow*. You can find this beginning in 2 Samuel 1:17 in the Old Testament.

Can I get through this alone?

Put simply, we're nuts if we think you can or should. Something happens to our whole chemistry during grief that makes it difficult to think clearly and wisely.

A favourite piece of wisdom of mine is this: *"Two are better than one because they have a good return for their labour. For if either of them falls, the one will lift up his companion. But woe to the one who falls when there is not another to lift him up."* (Ecclesiastes 4:9–10)

I made an almost-fatal financial mistake in the midst of grief that would have been easily solved if I'd had a wise and trustworthy third party to help me process my thinking. Prior to grief, I had been discerning and assessing to the point I had helped others avoid speculative and shaky "investment" opportunities. In grief, I became impulsive and risk-taking, just so I could have the feeling of "being alive" again. Here is what happened...

I received a small insurance payout following Marilyn's death. Prior to that, while pre-grieving, I convinced Marilyn to "invest" the insurance payout we received due to her illness in a scheme claiming to return between 20% and 30% on the investment. A close family friend alerted me to this opportunity and in the wash-up, they lost a truckload of money also.

> *Lesson one:* NEVER listen to the advice of close friends who are not qualified to give financial advice.
>
> *Lesson two:* If a financial scheme looks too good to be true, it nearly always is.
>
> *Lesson three:* If the people luring you into parting with your hard-earned dollars are not registered with ASIC, or the relevant government authority, steer clear.
>
> *Lesson four:* Never make these kinds of decisions alone, particularly in a season of grief. Your brain is only working on two and a half cylinders.
>
> *Lesson five:* Learn the difference between investing and speculating.
>
> *Lesson six:* Google "Ponzi Schemes". Learn to recognize them and avoid them like the bubonic plague.
>
> *Lesson seven:* Learn the basics regarding financial management and ensure they are operating successfully at home before you consider making larger decisions in ignorance. It is EVERY person's responsibility to understand financial management whether you're good at mathematics or not.

At this time, I had almost paid off my family home but those inspiring me to "invest" introduced me to the "eighth wonder of the world"... compounding interest. I have used inverted commas around the word "invest" because what I was doing was *not* investing, it was speculating. The common word for speculating is gambling, and in the midst of grief, I gambled away half the value of my family home, just to feel like I was alive.

I genuinely believed I was setting myself up for a productive future. I genuinely believed I was honouring God. If ONLY I had realised how vulnerable grief and ignorance were combining to make me.

In reality, I had placed my money into the hands of a thief and, the last time I looked, their job description was to TAKE money from vulnerable people. Because we are stewards, not owners of our finance, I later learned I had to apologise to God for squandering the wealth He had helped me accumulate. That set me up to recover from an extremely painful time.

The point is, I could have avoided this unnecessary drama by having a small group of trusted professionals who could be consulted before the launching of my own personal *Titanic*. I honestly shake my head in wonderment I have not gone down with the boat on so many previous occasions. My mum used to say: "David, if there's a hard way to do something, you'll find it."

I sometimes compare my life to my golf game: a series of miraculous recoveries!

Key Thoughts

Learn to recognise the difference between the questions that harm and those that help.

A male's greatest emotional need is acceptance.

Some men are just the marrying kind. In fact, the Bible says celibacy is a gift.

There is a time when you shouldn't remarry for the children's sake, and a time when you should.

Re–marrying at the right time tells everyone that, despite the pain of yesterday, you are moving forwards into your future.

One of life's greatest keys is that we tend to accept what we do understand and reject what we don't understand.

Think up one strong, consistent, simple confession about your future you can declare every day.

Grief is more about your lingering pain than about the one who died.

Body chemistry changes during grief, making it difficult to think clearly and wisely.

Avoid unnecessary dramas by having a small group of trusted professionals to consult in your decision–making.

CHAPTER SIX
UNKNOWINGLY PREPARED

"One generation's revelations are the next generation's discoveries."

Unknowingly, I was being prepared for my valley long before I entered it.

In 1968, at the Sydney Cricket Ground, I discovered there was a lot more to life than I had previously thought. I was sitting on the grass, listening to Billy Graham preaching. I certainly believed there was a God—thanks to my parent's involvement in the Anglican Church in Grafton. But I certainly was NOT there because of that.

Uh uh! I was there because a pretty girl had invited me and because I was once heard to say in my youth: "There would be no reason to live if it wasn't for cricket."

Two really powerful motivations to be at the SCG that night!

When the evangelist gave an invitation to come forwards and "give your life to Christ", I had no idea what he was talking about. Still, I felt as if my heart would beat clear out of my chest if I didn't.

I couldn't tell you what he preached about for those fifteen minutes because I was busy concentrating on the girl. And when people ask me today why I responded to Christ, I simply explain, "I couldn't help it."

From that time, I began to see what I had previously considered to be "life" was only a very small part of the total picture. Earth and life as we knew it was apparently only part of the whole of God's creation—with the bigger part hidden from view.

I had been spiritually blinded and alienated from God by sin. Previously, sin was what I used to boast about the morning after. Now it reappeared as the most powerful poison of all. I discovered I had been born with the horrible stuff, and forgiveness from God was the ONLY remedy.

Beyond natural sight, there was a "world" that God lived in, with other created beings I couldn't see or didn't know about. With that experience at the Sydney Cricket Ground, religion and Christianity had become personal.

Still today, having a relationship with the Creator of the universe blows me away. As it developed I discovered two doors in the Bible. The first was the one into my life.

"Behold, I stand at the door and knock; if anyone hears My voice and opens the door, I will come in to him and will dine with him, and he with Me." (Revelation 3:20)

The second was the doorway into His world.

"After these things I looked, and behold, a door standing open in heaven, and the first voice which I had heard, like the sound of a trumpet speaking with me, said, 'Come up here...'" (Revelation 4:1)

When Jesus was teaching His young disciples to pray, He had taught them about this door:

"But you, when you pray, go into your inner room, close your door and pray to your Father who is in secret, and your Father who sees what is done in secret will reward you." (Matthew 6:6)

Not to put too fine a point on it, it looked like there was a time when God wanted to come knocking on my front door, and times when He wanted me to come knocking on His.

It sounded like a mutual, reciprocating friendship.

Since the incident at the Sydney Cricket Ground, I have asked many people:

> "Where do you go when you pray?"
>
> "What happens when you pray?"
>
> "What do you see when you pray?"

I have had a wide range of answers. Some say they see a light. Others say they get a sense of being close to God. Many admit to prayer being a difficult, distant experience.

We need to get EVERY benefit Jesus paid for with his bloody crucifixion, and He described one of those benefits as an ability to "come to the Father".

I remember when I first discovered the doorway into His presence. It was a discovery perfectly illustrated in CS Lewis' book, *The Lion, the Witch and the Wardrobe*, where the children discovered that the door in the back of the wardrobe led them into whole new world.

After Marilyn and I had pioneered our church in Port Macquarie, I discovered I had a real challenge on my hands. Because I was the pastor, people came back to ME after they had been prayed for, if they hadn't received the answer we had prayed for.

I had to immediately search for a more effective prayer life and, after attending a couple of seminars, commenced practising on my hapless congregation. As I was praying for a person one day, I had a clear impression I should read Matthew 6:6.

Perceiving the devil would not be the one assisting me in prayer, I concluded it must be God. I read it there and then and commenced taking my first person into the inner room to meet with their Saviour and Heavenly Father. In the process of taking someone else into the inner room, I had discovered it myself. And, at that precise moment, I discovered the quality of intimacy Jesus paid for us to experience.

This is beautifully described by the writer of the letter to the Hebrews:

> *"And so, dear brothers and sisters, we can boldly enter heaven's Most Holy Place because of the blood of Jesus. By His death, Jesus opened a new and life–giving way through the curtain into the Most Holy Place. And since we have a great High Priest who rules over God's house, let us go right into the presence of God with sincere hearts fully trusting Him. For our guilty consciences have been sprinkled with Christ's blood to make us clean, and our bodies have been washed with pure water."*
> (Hebrews 10:19–22 New Living Translation)

I hate it when we live below our potential, and every generation needs to know that His presence is their potential in prayer.

What has this got to do with grief?

It's simple.

Now I had my own Garden of Eden to go to, even at my lowest moments. The word "Eden" means *delights* and He doesn't see it as a corruption of that place when we go there filled with depression. The first time I discovered this door (interestingly, Jesus once described Himself as "the door", so guess who's waiting for you just inside?) I asked God: "What is in that place?"

As I stepped in, I got the impression of a starry universe. This inner room seemed to have no walls, no floor and no ceiling.

It occurred to me that Abraham found his way here; so had Moses, so had David, so had Elijah.... and now I had found my way here too. There was room for everyone, even me! I have to say, that was a WOW moment.

Let me relate an experience to show you how real this place is.

Before Marilyn died, her mother Vera had declined with old age. She was a couple of days away from eternity. Many years of smoking cigarettes had left her with emphysema plus a range of other symptoms. By this time, one or two tumours had been removed from Marilyn's brain (courtesy of melanoma) and things weren't looking great for her, either.

But if anyone thought she was going to let her mum die without Jesus, they would have to think again! When Marilyn became a Christian, it thoroughly confused Vera. She had an old–fashioned idea that, if someone prayed for you, it meant you were close to death. So she avoided every offer we gave her in this regard like the plague. Fear and confusion had her in its grip.

She lay in the palliative care section of St George Hospital in Sydney, the smell and atmosphere of death hanging like a fog in every corner. Marilyn greeted her mum, who was miraculously coherent at the time and Vera, full of fear, exclaimed: "Marilyn, I died!"

"Don't be silly Mum, you're still here."

Something cautioned me that Vera could be telling the truth, so I encouraged Marilyn to believe her and roll with it.

After all, we had been praying for her, hadn't we? And God loved her more than we did.

"Mum," said Marilyn, "God doesn't want you to die without Jesus; will you ask Him to forgive you and come into your heart?"

At this question, every fear in Vera seemed to surface and she began to wildly throw her head around in an agonised way. It appeared that unseen forces were tormenting her.

From the end of the bed, I said, "Marilyn, rebuke the enemy!"

With that, this tenacious little lady, with her own body fighting the merciless ravages of cancer, went to war. She put her head down next to her mother's ear and began to rebuke demons with the violence of a cornered lioness.

Now it stands to reason that, if a loving prayer freaked Vera out, this should have had her crawling across the ceiling. But no! Vera became as calm as a millpond. A supernatural peace descended onto her body and mind.

"Lead her to Jesus," I encouraged.

"Mum, can you see Jesus?" Marilyn asked.

"I can see Him," she responded.

"Where is He, what is He doing?"

"He is standing at the end of the bed, with His arms out, wanting me to come to Him." Vera was captivated by what she could see, and all fear had left. Right on her deathbed, she made the ultimate discovery.

"Time to lead her to Jesus," I nudged.

Marilyn said, "Look at Him and say this to Him. Jesus, I am a sinner. You are my Saviour. Please forgive me for every sin. I receive You now."

And after repeating those words with laboured breath, Vera soon lapsed back into unconsciousness and, a few days later, slipped out of her body into His waiting arms.

Life is meant to be a two–dimensional experience, where we are just as at home in God's world as we are in our own. When Vera's great challenge came, it was this that gave her the great discovery of her own Garden of Eden where she met her Lord and experienced peace even in the midst of death.

Can you see how valuable that kind of relationship with God could be in the midst of deep grief?

THIS is the preparation we need for any and every one of life's trials.

Everyone needs to know how he or she has been put together. The Maker's manual does that very plainly. He describes us as a spirit, soul and body. It's in 1 Thessalonians 5:23.

Our souls consist of things like our mind, will, emotions and intellect. It is in this area of our lives we can experience the emotional highs and lows of life. Together with rejection, unforgiveness, fear of rejection and guilt, grief is one of the most acute pains anyone can experience. When we invite the living God to heal and restore our souls, it results in a life full of perspective and wholeness, and we become able to navigate through the darkest of valleys.

It's never too late to discover this dimension to life. I am one of those who will never stop thanking God for helping me make this discovery.

Key Thoughts

Not to put too fine a point on it, it looked like there was a time when God wanted to come knocking on my front door, and times when He wanted me to come knocking on His.

We need to get EVERY benefit Jesus paid for with his bloody crucifixion.

Every generation needs to know that His presence is their potential in prayer.

Everyone needs to have his or her own Garden of Eden to go to, even at their lowest moments.

Life is meant to be a two–dimensional experience, where we are just as at home in God's world as we are in our own.

CHAPTER SEVEN
AVOIDING TEMPTATION WHILE GRIEVING

There are many traps waiting for us in a season of grief. As previously mentioned, I was easily conned into parting with my money. In hindsight, I learned that, during grief, our defences are down and that makes us highly vulnerable to tempting offers.

I have seen a number of forms of temptation. Every type promises you will "feel" better if you pursue it.

> *Food.* The sensation of beautiful flavours passing over your taste buds gives you momentary sweetness. But a little voice on the inside lets you know that the food when coupled with low motivation to exercise, will add unwanted and depressing kilos to your weight.
>
> *Pornography.* The images excite your bruised and lacerated soul, but you know the indulgence is spoiling the health of your inner man.

Spending. Whatever you buy brightens you up for the moment, but you know the pleasures you are experiencing will wear off very quickly.

This is where a "running mate" is vital. Someone we can be transparent with and accountable to. Someone non-judgmental who will spend time with us discussing issues that really matter.

Personally, I think we would benefit from actually paying a counselor or life/grief coach to fill this role. THIS purchase will be far more rewarding and satisfying than falling hook, line and sinker for the temptations our weakened souls can fall into.

The temptation to isolate when grieving can be a REALLY strong one for males. Grief plus isolation often results in emotional disaster.

The Australian male, and most males I would suggest, has a very powerful cultural weakness. What gives this weakness even greater power to harm is that it is generally thought of as a strength.

British tradition and Hollywood combine to paint a picture of men who can sustain any amount of pressure on their own... men portrayed as heroes for their ability to stand alone while others crumble around them... men who internalise all their emotions and somehow become their own counselor and coach, successfully holding things together... men who have resolute faces, set jaws, lips without a hint of a quiver, a steely gaze, quick thinking and an ability to hold it together.

IF ONLY IT WERE TRUE!

If only you had seen me at my weakest and most mistake-prone moments. Hollywood wouldn't have considered me for a starring role in some hyped-up movie.

This cultural weakness is ISOLATION, soldiering on alone. Rather than being physically, mentally and emotionally strong during grief, the norm is more like the following.

A big temptation for men (and for many women I suspect) is to sulk when we can't have what we want.

And what do we want? We want our wife back, and we want our sex life back, and we want... well, you complete the list for yourself.

Sulking can be the ultimate "me–centred" response. With great embarrassment, I confess to being guilty of having this as a personal indulgence in the early years of my first marriage. Is there anything less manly than a grown man acting like a four year old? One of the inescapable things about being a Christian is that God, who sees all, will not entertain the existence of things like this in any of His kids when they are so foreign to His own nature. He simply will not cohabit with this kind of immaturity. For our sakes, He helps us deal with it.

I used to be a classic sulker when my sexual needs were put on hold. Now most men will understand that they become the masters of bad timing when the testosterone in their chemistry gives them the green light.

"Gentlemen, start your engines!" says the little man in the Daytona racing car simulator. A couple of days before, you would have been a more coherent thinker. Now, however, the question you pose to your wife as to the time and location of your next sexual rendezvous sounds unreasonably mystifying to her, if not downright stupid.

This was the state of affairs on one occasion many years ago. The usual pattern was playing itself out. The sulker had been asked to be reasonable and had promptly declared a state of war. This was followed by the predictable stand–off.

Sulking really makes a man highly unattractive. What woman wants to fall into the arms of a boiling, heavy thundercloud, intent on using the art of sulking to exact revenge on her?

So I did what many men do. I ISOLATED.

In that moment of genius, with my rejection and thoughts to myself, God decided I needed some help. As I began praying, I could see my reaction was abnormal, given the size of the problem. After all, Marilyn had only said, "Wait." I wasn't the victim of rejection at all. Little problem, huge reaction! And I began to see that my situation was more than emotional... there must have been a spiritual element to it.

I have come to learn over the years that demons are real. I have also come to see they camouflage themselves in natural circumstances and are thereby deceptive. They hide in circumstances and situations where they can remain undetected.

Incidentally, that is what the word "occult" means: *hidden*. I concluded that, whereas the problem was only the size of a tennis ball, a great cloud of bull–dust consisting of lies, exaggerations, innuendoes, accusations and anger had been kicked up, making it look like the explosion of a nuclear warhead.

And so I further concluded I could more easily deal with the problem if I removed the cloud of bull–dust and brought it down to its real, tennis–ball size.

I was reading the gospel of Luke at the time and learned something that has helped me ever since. *"Any kingdom divided against itself is laid waste; and a house divided against itself falls. If Satan also is divided against himself, how will his kingdom stand?"* (Luke 11:17)

Rather than have the enemy divide us, my victory lay in dividing them. So I just pulled that verse out of its holster, loaded my mouth with it and shot it time and time again into the kingdom of darkness. With those shots, I was picking off the demonic beings that had been arrayed against my precious marriage.

And guess what happened?

Nothing.

Or so I thought. I was disappointed to say the least. I was still upset. So I lay down for half an hour without sleeping, only to experience this stuff being progressively leached out of my soul. With my mind now functioning WITHOUT being engulfed in that horrible pressure, I was able to repent for my unreasonable attitudes, restore our relationship without fuss, and walk away with another victorious strategy for happiness under my belt.

Marilyn didn't believe it at first. A rapid turn around like this had to be suspected.

Try it. When, in the midst of grief, you begin feeling like the victim, do this. Consult your counselor or life coach, who should also be your prayer partner, your running mate.

Find a verse that speaks of victory over the enemy, load it into your mouth and open fire mercilessly on the kingdom of darkness. It has no mercy on you. You won't find any sympathy there because you're grieving. Oh no... he wants to lay the boot in while you're down. The name of Jesus on a grieving person's lip is just as powerful as on anyone else's. The kingdom of darkness will be divided and be rendered powerless, and you will continue grieving successfully.

Let me give you a loving challenge as we close this chapter. You can give yourself permission to grieve without giving yourself permission to sulk. Grieving is different to playing the victim. It is different to cowardice. So come on out of your man cave (or woman cave), if you're in there and start grieving with courage!

Key Thoughts

We would benefit from actually paying a counselor or life/grief coach.

The temptation to isolate when grieving can be a REALLY strong one for males.

Sulking can be the ultimate 'me–centred' response.

\# Sulking really makes a man (or anyone for that matter) appear highly unattractive.

\# Demons camouflage themselves in natural circumstances.

\# The name of Jesus on a grieving person's lip is just as powerful as on anyone else's.

\# You can give yourself permission to grieve without giving yourself permission to sulk.

CHAPTER EIGHT
CHOOSING A MATE SECOND TIME AROUND

Almost thirty years of marriage had not made me an expert in choosing a wife for the second time. The real truth was I felt like a novice.

When I was first married, I didn't have a broken heart, and I wasn't recovering from the loss of my covenant mate. So how could I entertain the prospect of having a new mate while the previous one was still so alive in my heart?

I felt challenged to do something that was extremely difficult. The love I had received from Marilyn was rich, rewarding and accepting. It became obvious I was being challenged to let it slip away just like in the epic movie *Titanic*, Leonardo DiCaprio slipped out of Kate Winslet's reach, swallowed by the waters of the Atlantic.

Letting go of that love with only the possibility of it being resurrected with re–marriage was a big ask. And who knew if it would play out that way? I didn't know how God would fill the void if I surrendered it fully to Him.

As I contemplated this, my soul predicted a great emptiness for a long time, possibly an unbearable one. And yet somewhere within, I wanted to trust God for His miraculous provision. I felt totally out of my depth.

Twelve weeks after her death, I began by saying my goodbyes to Marilyn a little bit more everyday. Does that make sense? Something this big could only happen by degrees. I suspect this allowed me to meditate on what the future could look like, and I began to think of the differences in a marriage second time around.

1. The unlikelihood of having children.
2. The possibility of being a step-parent.
3. Having a family tree on both sides of the marriage.
4. A significant part of both our destinies had already been lived out.
5. Established work patterns.
6. Established routines, habits and preferences.
7. Ownership of accumulated property and possessions.
8. Existing family responsibilities.
9. Lifelong friendships already established for both of us.
10. Both have already experienced a covenant, "until death us do part" marriage.
11. Gaining approval of your potential new mate from your children.

The first marriage had prepared me personally; hopefully I was a more mature person. But this journey looked decidedly different than the first.

It can feel like you are betraying your mate, even though he or she is no longer there, even by thinking of the possibility of another marriage. So I did something to make sure these false emotions had no hold over me.

I had placed Marilyn's ashes in a memorial garden about half an hour away. Off I headed for the very first time. I drove slower and slower the closer I got, realising by degrees the difficulty involved in doing it. I slowly found the place I had chosen to place her ashes overlooking a pond, checked to see if anyone was near and then let my emotions flow. Others came and went. I saw them walk past another man who was sitting on the grass as near as possible to the person he loved.

I sat and talked to Marilyn about a conflict that had occurred with Belinda that morning. I told her how much I missed her and asked whether I should head towards re-marriage. We discussed everything as a couple, and a decision as important as this required joint input. It was too early to resolve this question, but it felt good to talk about it and include Marilyn in the equation. I must have spent over an hour there. Leaving was painfully difficult. Bed felt wonderful that night, stinging eyes, headaches and all. Including Marilyn in this conversation silenced the voices accusing me of betrayal.

Later, I came to realise Marilyn had no further use of marriage. She had been completed the moment she met her heavenly bridegroom. Today I joke about her leaving me for another man and (with my full approval) not wanting to come back. I, however, (with her full approval) DID have a need for marriage. Do you ever wonder if people in eternity can see back into time? I think they can, and I think Marilyn is cheering me on in my new marriage, wanting Tuula and I to enjoy all the love it is possible to experience. The truth was, she had "gained" according to that wonderful verse Paul wrote to the Philippians: *"For to me, to live is Christ and to die is gain."* (Philippians 1:21)

Marilyn, through death, had gained an immeasurable amount. If I were to gain another wife, this "gain" would be far less than Marilyn's. So re-marriage for me would become a win–win, rather than staying alone and experiencing a win–lose.

During the first twelve months, I met a number of "possibles"... wonderful ladies who could have been the future Mrs. Schaeffer. "Could this be the one?" Don't be embarrassed to know that this question can crop up often. When considering this question I read this wisdom: *"And I discovered more bitter than death the woman whose heart is snares and nets, whose hands are chains. One who is pleasing to God will escape from her, but the sinner will be captured by her."* (Ecclesiastes 7:26)

The girls I met were lovely and their hearts were far from being "snares and nets" but the verse was a warning to me there were disastrous consequences attached to teaming up with the wrong mate. There was a woman planned for me before I was born. I like the idea that, despite the fact that we meet, fall in love, and take responsibility for our choices, it is still pre–planned (versus "arranged").

I liked the idea of falling in love again, but the consequences of being rash and impulsive rather than considered and prayerful according to Ecclesiastes 7:26 were frightening. I considered myself warned.

And so after a small number of brief friendships, safely seen through by a transparent and accountable relationship with a reliable and wise mentor, I went to the Bible to see if God had anything to say to me about a future mate. I needed wisdom, so why would I look somewhere else for something inferior?

I turned to the Book of Ruth in the Old Testament. Why? It just occurred to me to do so. No angelic appearances, no heavenly choir. In it, I read about a woman who

> \# Was born in another country and culture.
>
> \# Had lost her first husband.
>
> \# Had relocated in and adopted another country as her own.
>
> \# Had strong family ties in her extended family.
>
> \# Was attracted to an older man.
>
> \# Was bold and went after the man she wanted.
>
> \# Took initiative and had an upbeat approach to life even in a downtime.

\# Knew the definition of commitment.

\# Made choices that led her to be included by God in His history book.

Many people know the following statement: it came from the lips of Ruth the Moabitess: *"Do not urge me to leave you or turn back from following you; for where you go, I will go, and where you lodge, I will lodge. Your people shall be my people, and your God, my God. Where you die, I will die, and there I will be buried. Thus may the Lord do to me, and worse, if anything but death parts you and me."* (Ruth 1:16–17)

If anyone thinks I believed this was a direct message from God to me, they'd be quite wrong. By this time, my brain had begun to work again and the wise counsel I had received over the previous twelve months had helped me get things back in perspective.

The truth was, I refused to believe it simply because I didn't trust my grieving soul to know if it was God or merely an exciting idea. So I did what Mary did when the twelve year old Jesus was found asking questions of Church leaders during a visit to Jerusalem. *"And His mother treasured all these things in her heart."* (Luke 2:51)

I simply put them up on the shelf and kept doing my best to live wisely every day.

In a matter of months, I received an email from a girl who had been brushing across my mind often enough in the days preceding its arrival. That got me a little interested. Tuula had been divorced prior to my bereavement and had sent me a condolence card along with hundreds from others. I remember she had included her phone number on it and, at the time, I can remember thinking how forward that was. When you get to know Tuula, you understand that she wasn't being forward at all. She is a genuinely confident, warm, friendly person.

What was I to do? We exchanged a number of emails before a conference was being held at the Sydney Olympic Complex. I entertained the idea of her being there, but confidently dismissed those thoughts as she was attending a church in a different denomination.

My good friend Kev sidled up to me on the night with one of his sly grins. "Look who's here."

What happened next changed my views on the possibility of love at first sight. We had a coffee with her son Ariel after the meeting, but I couldn't wait to see Kevin and Di the next day and demand, "What have you done with my head?"

They just giggled, pleaded ignorance and innocence, and left me in my confusion.

Further emails were followed by our first date during Easter 2005. We were both attracted to each other, but a couple of things really worried me. I was fully aware of the dangers of cross-generational and cross-cultural relationships, and these became strong discussion points between us. Our eleven-year gap in ages worried me a lot more than it did her, and she proved to be truly bi-cultural, slotting as easily into Aussie culture as her native Finland (Tuula had emigrated with her family when she was ten). Minus twenty and minus thirty degrees are easy to leave for the sunshine of the Great Southland!

At some point after we had charted our path towards marriage, I remembered what I had read in the book of Ruth. I ticked every box and sat in amazement and realized that God, in His own amazing way, had indeed spoken to me. That became strong confirmation that our choice of each other was perfect.

The battle for a new life wasn't over at this point—it was just beginning. But now I would have a covenant mate as my companion in battle. Some time later, we were asked to speak at a marriage and family seminar as a couple who had navigated some serious rocks in the river. We divided our presentation into four parts:

> # Single again: Bereavement and Divorce

\# Bankruptcy and Financial Crisis (Tuula was bankrupt when we met)

\# Married Again

\# The Blended Family.

We could not believe we had not only survived, but were really continuing to win the battle for our own and for our children's happiness.

Key Thoughts

\# The second marriage is a very different journey to the first.

\# Your first wife has no further use of marriage, but you may.

\# There are disastrous consequences attached to teaming up with the wrong mate.

\# Don't trust yourself to hear Gods voice during a time of grief. Your soul can attach itself to anything that sounds like good news.

\# Be aware of the dangers of cross–generational and cross–cultural relationships.

CHAPTER NINE
TRUSTING GOD AGAIN

Very early in Tuula's and my friendship, she made the statement that many people make following bereavement and/or divorce: "I don't know if I can trust God again."

When we first stepped out in our walk with God, we had no inkling that pain of such magnitude would occur. In this we were like many others, despite the fact it is happening to people all around the world, every day. We innocently believed that, because God is a good God, He would cause good things to happen to us. Then, out of the blue, something we never imagined, and never planned for, happened.

Experience followed experience and we began to get the idea God was not going to shield us from life's harm and pain. In fact, we began to understand there are times when He would lead us through painful experiences to show others going through the same thing how differently someone walking with God does it.

I have since coined the phrase 'God is far more concerned with our destiny than He is with our happiness.' Part of our destiny is to walk through the same things others walk through and come out whole, as well as stronger, and richer for the experience. When others cannot find God, they could observe Him helping us get better while they may be getting bitter.

I think I went from being an adolescent Christian to an adult Christian when that sank in.

In the midst of working this out, I was enjoying a meal in Sydney with my good friend Geoff Woodward. 'What differences have these experiences made in your relationship with God?' he asked between mouthfuls.

'To be honest,' I answered, ' I keep looking over my shoulder for the next slap I'm not expecting.' My answer troubled me because it revealed I was not back at full trust again. I was being cautious about trusting Him fully. Somewhere beneath the surface of my life, I considered God an unpredictable and dangerous father and friend. All my Christian life I thought I could trust Him without question, but now I wasn't sure.

Ross Abraham, Chairman of INC Oceania, shares this remarkable insight regarding Job, a character in the Old Testament who suffered extreme loss and grief: *"The root of his pain was not the loss of his possessions, but the perceived loss of God's presence."*

There can be a lot of pain in our hearts even after we have reconciled that the one we loved has left our address and moved on... forever! It's one thing to lose sight of someone you deeply loved, and quite another to lose sight of God.

For me, this matter of trust was resolved in stages.

First, I came to see I hadn't understood how God walks with us and that there are occasions when He allows pain and suffering. 'For goodness sake,' I reasoned, 'EVERYONE dies'.

Further to that, He can allow it without warning. It is His prerogative whether He warns us or not. However I suspect there are times when He wants to give us no advantage over another person trying to walk the grief journey alone and without God. Our example to them at that time can be hope for them at a hopeless time. Honestly, is there anything more inspiring than a Christian in full flight?

Charles Spurgeon is quoted as saying: *"When you can't trace His hand, you must learn to trust His heart."*

The songwriter Barry Mann added this verse to Robert Browning Hamilton's timeless poem cited at the beginning of this book.

> *"The frost is in the valley and the mountain tops turn grey.*
>
> *The promised buds all wither and blossoms fade away.*
>
> *Our loving Father whispers, 'All this comes from my hand,*
>
> *And blessed are you when you trust, when you just can't understand.'"*

Secondly, I also saw how He had watched over me and provided perfectly for my kids and me through the process. I will never stop thanking God for bringing Tuula and Chris and Heather Freeman (my life coach and friend) into my life to play such an astonishingly wonderful part of my restoration.

Thirdly, understanding the principle of stewardship is a vital ingredient in processing grief successfully. This principle states that we are the managers of everything and the owners of nothing. Job, in the Old Testament, initially summed up his experience like this. *"The Lord gave and the Lord has taken away."* (Job 1:21)

When we understand that we do not own our time, finance, possessions and relationships, we are able to bow to the plan the real owner has for these same things. It is not a foreign concept. Most of us have heard the platitude "our children are only given to us for a short time" and accepted it. The same truth applies to wives and husbands. At what point in your marriage did you begin "owning" your wife or husband?

Fourthly, as Ross Abraham pointedly states, *"Brokenness always precedes usefulness."*

Is it possible you will be infinitely more useful to the occupants of planet earth during and following your recovery? Could it be that grieving with hope is an act of worship, stating wordlessly that things won't always be this way?

These days happily, I am back to full trust with added wisdom.

Key Thoughts

We tend to innocently believe that, because God is a good God, He would only cause good things to happen to us.

God is far more concerned with our destiny than He is with our happiness.

There are occasions when God allows serious pain and suffering.

It's one thing to lose sight of someone you deeply loved, and quite another to lose sight of God.

Understanding the principle of stewardship is a vital ingredient in processing grief successfully.

At what point in your marriage did you begin "owning" your wife or husband?

Could it be that grieving with hope is an act of worship, stating wordlessly that things won't always be this way?

Brokenness always precedes usefulness.

CHAPTER TEN
GRIEVE UPWARDS

"A good name is better than a good ointment,
and the day of one's death is better than the day of one's birth.
It is better to go to a house of mourning
than to go to a house of feasting,
because that is the end of every man,
and the living takes it to heart.
Sorrow is better than laughter,
for when a face is sad a heart may be happy.
The mind of the wise is in the house of mourning,
while the mind of fools is in the house of pleasure."

Ecclesiastes 7:1–4

Patient, professional, motherly, discerning, calm and calming, brilliant in every way: these are only some adjectives that could describe Belinda's physician, Simone Strasser at Sydney's Royal Prince Alfred Hospital. Simone was associated with every fear, challenge and uncertainty prior to Bel's liver transplant and life afterwards. She was a rock to us all. Belinda's condition once prompted her to exclaim, "The words 'Belinda' and 'normal' do *NOT* fit in the same sentence." Her best was our blessing. She had helped to give us years with Bel we might not have had otherwise, right up to the moment at hand.

When the nurse pulled the curtain around Belinda's bed in the intensive care section at Royal Prince Alfred Hospital in the inner Sydney suburb of Camperdown, crunch time had arrived. All other family and friends graciously withdrew to allow Rohan, Belinda's husband of fifteen months, and myself, Bel's dad, to be there with her for this numbing moment. With her immune system lowered to enable her body to retain a transplanted liver, a rare and aggressive form of cancer, like a bushfire, had mercilessly swept through.

And now we had to let her go.

Have you ever wondered what it would be like to make the decision to have the life support turned off from someone you deeply loved? I had. And now here it was, a reality being played out before our very eyes.

Some four years earlier another family had not only been through this overwhelming experience, but had also given permission for the healthy organs of their loved one to be removed and placed into the dying body of another to give it life. There are no words to express our gratitude.

I remember seeing on video the liver they removed from Belinda before transplanting the donated one. I thought: *someone needs to pin a medal on it*. It was greenish, misshapen and ugly. It was a miracle that it had supported Belinda's body for twenty–eight years!

There she lay now with all kinds of tubes in her hands and neck, connecting her to a variety of machines that maintained a heartbeat and pulse. Was she still with us? Or had she already left? The poor, beautiful nurse asked if we were ok to proceed.

No, we weren't.

And yes, we were.

And one by one, she disconnected the supply lines of life to Belinda's wasted, tiny frame.

What *really* happens to someone when they die? Paul, the premier writer in the New Testament boils it down to this simple equation:

> *"Therefore, being always of good courage, and knowing that while we are at home in the body we are absent from the Lord— for we walk by faith, not by sight—we are of good courage, I say, and prefer rather to be absent from the body and to be at home with the Lord."* (2 Corinthians 5:6–8)

Absent here, present there. This cuts through every complicated, confused philosophy and theory.

It is totally believable because the same Person who re–appeared for forty days after being publicly crucified just outside the City of Jerusalem, had then met Paul (then named Saul), rescued him from his perverted thinking, and explained the realities of life, death and eternity to him. The change in Paul's life wasn't remarkable, it was miraculous... even impossible. Darkness to light stuff. Blindness to sight. Deaf to hearing. 180 degrees the other way.

Everyone has to face death sometime. We should consider how to best prepare for the event.

I once read about a man who built a coffin, sat it up on two sawhorses in the garage where there was a nice breeze, and had a nap in it every Saturday afternoon. He even had his wife take photographs of him! Some preparation!

Belinda had somewhat–faced and somewhat–avoided it all her life. Before her nine–hour transplant operation, she wrote us individual letters just in case she didn't survive the operation. Oh, she was a courageous little thing! With a flick of the elastic band around her surgical shower cap, she gave us one of her wicked little grins and headed away on the gurney into the operating theatre. I had given her a final hug and whispered: "Now you go in there and have the time of your life!"

This was all being filmed of course. Some time before, Bel and her younger sister Rachel had been presented with the opportunity to have the transplant journey recorded for all Australia to see on Channel Nine's *RPA* program.

Well, the opportunity to become reality TV stars was way too tempting and these two outrageous chicky babes were officially in their element! Obviously, there is an upside to everything.

Carol and Penny, producers and directors of the program, together with the whole TV crew adopted Belinda as one of their own. Coffees would arrive in the ward during her convalescence and "mother" Carol would take Belinda's washing home. I don't know if they realise yet that they were amazing gifts of God to my little girl. Sometimes we go through so much turmoil we miss seeing the things a loving Father provides just to see us through.

You have to be well enough and sick enough to receive an organ transplant. Belinda was quite close to death, perhaps weeks, perhaps months, prior to the operation. "Miss Schaeffer," children in her class would ask, "can you see in the dark?" Her jaundiced eyes were roughly the same colour as an orange traffic light… like a cat's eyes in the dark.

Marriage for Belinda was fairytale stuff. When she was giving her speech at the wedding reception, she shared she had never been able to dream of a husband or family because life had presented too many challenges and uncertainties. I realised for the first time I had never been able to have that dream for her either.

But here she was, dressed as a princess, marrying a prince who would love her completely every day of their covenant life together.

She shared another interesting thing during her speech also. When Belinda was a little girl, we would have to go into her bedroom while she was sleeping to give her a gooey mixture of *Questran*, which among other things reduced the itching associated with liver disease.

It was often my task to semi–awaken her and shovel it into her mouth. After this was done, I would spend a little extra time speaking life-giving words over her. "You will grow up to be a great woman of God, wise and beautiful," I would say. "You will become a high achiever in all you do. You will grow healthy and strong." Sometimes I would sense a flow of words as if I was being divinely helped to speak what she needed to receive.

When I was saying these things, Belinda pretended to be asleep, but was awake, absorbing every word.

Belinda's death was my eighth season of deep grief. At the time of writing, we are a little less than a year into the experience, so while the pages may feel dry to you, they are still a little moist with our tears. One would be excused for surmising that, after eight doses of grief, a person really should be some sort of wreck, a piece of flotsam washed up on life's shore.

Quite the opposite!

A wonderful Heavenly Dad has walked me through each season of loss, strengthening me a little more each time and helping me gain an eternal perspective on things. Let me share a secret with you.

I have discovered that, when this is a shared experience with the Author of Life, the closer we get to death, the more brushes with it we have, the less it scares us. Paul puts it like this: *"For our dying bodies must be transformed into bodies that will never die; our mortal bodies must be transformed into immortal bodies. Then, when our dying bodies have been transformed into bodies that will never die, this Scripture will be fulfilled:*
> *'Death is swallowed up in victory.*
> *O death, where is your victory?*
> *O death, where is your sting?'"*
>   (1 Corinthians 15:53–55 New Living Translation)

Here is the truth. We all live, we all die, and then we all live forever. What a wonderful truth Jesus gave us! His message of salvation contains a survival kit for death itself!

And how do we make sense of the rotten things that happen to us? How did Belinda?

Simple.

In the words of Christopher Reeve who once acted in the role of *Superman*, only to have an accident and become a quadriplegic, "You play the cards you are dealt."

Where was God when Belinda needed Him?

Available.

Right where He is when *YOU* need Him.

If His choice for us is to go through things rather than around them, there will be a purpose in it. Belinda demonstrated that a relationship with God is not dependent on having all good things happen. She was a beacon of light to everyone else whose life–experiences weren't fair. So if "life sucks" for you, invite your new available Friend in and see if you don't begin winning in your thoughts and attitudes.

And what is my personal summary of life? Well, most days I'm the happiest bloke I know. Why? Because

> *"It is the blessing of the Lord that makes rich,*
> *And He adds no sorrow to it."* (Proverbs 10:22)

Like many others, I have had plenty of sorrow but none of it has stuck. I've been made rich in the truth, and the sorrow I have experienced has been swallowed up by it. I have been bruised and healed, just as this astonishingly beautiful verse in Isaiah says:

> *"A bruised reed He will not break*
> *And a dimly burning wick He will not extinguish..."*
> (Isaiah 42:3)

And you know something? Bel's grave is only a couple of hundred metres beyond my back fence. I only go there now and again, for two reasons:

1. She's not there.
2. I have another place to go... through a doorway into an inner room where there is comfort laid on. I can't see them yet but EVERYONE who has loved Christ during the history of the human race is there, including Bel.

So... instead of grieving downwards into an abyss of unresolved sadness and questions, GRIEVE UPWARDS into the loving arms of God, where you will be re-made into a person of beauty and strength.

Key Thoughts

It is better to go to a house of mourning than to go to a house of feasting, because that is the end of every man, and the living takes it to heart.

Absent here, present there. This cuts through every complicated, confused philosophy and theory.

Everyone has to face death sometime. We should consider how to best prepare for the event.

Sometimes we go through so much turmoil that we miss seeing the things a loving Father gives us to see us through.

One would be excused for surmising that, after multiple doses of grief, a person really should be some sort of wreck, a piece of flotsam washed up on life's shore. Quite the opposite!

The closer we get to death, the more brushes with it we have, the less it scares us.

Here is the truth. We all live, we all die, and then we all live forever. What a wonderful truth Jesus gave us! His message of salvation contains a survival kit for death itself!

Where was God when Belinda needed Him? Available, right where He is when *YOU* need Him.

Instead of grieving downwards into an abyss of unresolved sadness and questions, GRIEVE UPWARDS.

EPILOGUE

You are still here because it's not your turn yet.

If your marriage covenant was an intimate, close bond that grew richer with time, you probably feel as if most things that were good about you just died with your mate.

If it was something else or less, you are faced just the same, with the empty prospect of living the remainder of your days with your mate sheared away from you.

The future is once again a blank canvass, waiting for you to take up your brush and begin the new work. And you have no inclination or energy to even pick up the brush.

I hope my story encourages you to hang on, walk with God and experience all the good things that are laid out for you ahead. I like what Sir Winston Churchill once said,

"History will be kind to me for I intend to write it."

Enjoy writing the next chapters of your life!

ENDNOTES

1. Linn, D., Linn, M., & Fabricant, S. (1985) *Healing the Greatest Hurt*, pp 8, Mahwah, NJ: Paulist Press.
2. Sleith, E, lll. (1984). *Embracing and Transcending Death, Loss. & Grief*, pp 1, Lincoln. NE: iUniverse Inc.
3. Bowlby, J. (1980). *Attachment and Loss: Vol.3. Loss: Sadness and Depression,* pp 399, New York: Basic Books.
4. Kubler–Ross, E., & Kessler, D. *On Grief and Grieving,* pp 25, London: Simon & Schuster.
5. Dunn, B., & Leonard, K. (2004). *Through a Season of Grief: Devotions for Your Journey from Mourning to Joy*, pp 8, USA: Thomas Nelson.

ABOUT THE AUTHOR

At the age of eighteen, David's father, a WW2 fighter pilot, died in his early fifties from a heart attack. Since then he has experienced seven further seasons of grief, two of which concerned his first wife and eldest daughter. While studying agriculture, his life was radically interrupted at a Billy Graham Crusade in 1968. In 1980 he left the agricultural scene in pursuit of his growing passion, people.

In Christian Outreach Centre (now International Network of Churches), David became a Senior Pastor, Church planter, District Chairman, State Chairman and National Executive member, spanning thirty-eight years. He currently mentors Church pastors and their leadership teams; is a BWC personal management coach and grief coach. He conducts Safe Church workshops, and is a volunteer pastor at Empower Church, in Castle Hill, Sydney. He lives in the nearby suburb of Kellyville Ridge with his beautiful wife Tuula.

INVITE DAVID TO SPEAK TO YOUR GROUP OR GATHERING

David is a gifted communicator and story teller, experienced in assisting people one on one or in small or large group settings. He will help people to see their grief in perspective and encourage them to go forwards with courage and hope, inspiring them to believe that they have the inner resources to make what looks difficult, if not impossible, possible.

All who hear him will leave with an upward perspective, believing there is life after death and loss.

You can contact David at www.davidschaeffer.com.au to discuss how he could partner with you in restoring lives.

www.ingramcontent.com/pod-product-compliance
Lightning Source LLC
Chambersburg PA
CBHW061459040426
42450CB00008B/1416